T0197118

THE
SUPERHEROES
MOVIES
TRIVIA QUIZ BOOK

Print and eBooks by M.A. Cassata

(Published as Mary Anne Cassata)

The Essential Jim Carrey
The Cher Scrapbook
The Elton John Scrapbook
The 'NSync Handbook
The Lil' Bow Wow Scrapbook
The Official Dance Party USA Book
The Britney Spears Handbook
Meet Jim Carrey
Hey, Hey, We're The Monkees
The Star Address Book
The Year of Michael J. Fox
Cher!

(Published as M. A. Cassata)

The Elton John Scrapbook: Revised and Updated Edition
Ross Lynch: Facts, Quizzes, Quotes 'N' More!
The Vamps: Facts, Quizzes, Quotes 'N' More!
*On The Teen Beat's Awesome Star Contact List and
     Birthday*
Ariana Grande: Fun Facts, Stats, Quizzes, Quotes 'N' More!
Big Time Rush: Fun Facts, Stats, Quizzes and Quotes
The Essential Cher, Vol. 1
One Direction: Fun Facts, Stats, Quizzes and Quotes
The Essential Jim Carrey

THE
SUPERHEROES
MOVIES
TRIVIA QUIZ BOOK

UNOFFICIAL AND UNAUTHORIZED

M.A. CASSATA

THE SUPERHEROES MOVIES TRIVIA QUIZ BOOK
UNOFFICIAL AND UNAUTHORIZED

iUniverse books may be ordered through booksellers or by contacting:

iUniverse
1663 Liberty Drive
Bloomington, IN 47403
www.iuniverse.com
1-800-Authors (1-800-288-4677)

ISBN: 978-1-5320-2932-5 (sc)
ISBN: 978-1-5320-2933-2 (e)

Print information available on the last page.

iUniverse rev. date: 08/11/2017

DEDICATION

To all the serious superhero movie fans in the world. I hope you find this ebook as entertaining as it is both fun and informative.

* * *

INTRODUCTION

Here are 160 questions about many of your favorite movie superheroes and even a few villains thrown in for good measure. Test your wits! Find out how well you know these big screen superhero movie characters. Above all, have fun!

* * *

QUIZ #1 QUESTIONS

1. Who is Selina Kyle in *The Dark Knight*?

2. True or False. The ring on Mandarin's finger is the same one Raza wore in the first *Iron Man* film.

3. Fill in the blank from *Captain America: Civil War*.

    Nick Fury: "S.H.I.E.L.D. takes the world as it is, not as we'd like it to be."
    Steve Rogers: _____.

4. How many hours of make-up was Alan Cumming forced to endure to become Nightcrawler for church scene in *X-Men 2*?

    a) 5
    b) 2
    c) 10
    d) 4

5. Fill in the blank from *Batman Begins* (2005).
    Jim Gordon: "I never said thank you."
    Batman: "_____."

6. What year was depicted in the beginning of *Ant-Man* (2015)?

a) 1989
b) 1987
c) 1985
d) 1984

7. True or False. In *The Wolverine* (2013), Yukio and Viper are mutants and Harada is not. In the comic they are the opposite.

8. True or False: An early draft of Iron Man revealed Tony Stark to be the creator of Dr. Otto Octavius's tentacles from believe it or not, *Spider-Man 2* in 2004.

9. What is the Vampire Bible referred to in *Blade* (1998)?

10. Fill in the blank from Iron Man 3.
    The Mandarin: "You don't know who I am. You'll never see me coming. My soldiers are coming. So run away, hide, because nothing can save you!"
    Tony Stark: "_____"

11. True or False in *Green Lantern* (2011), Superman had a cameo as one of candidates considered to receive a power ring.

12. Where were all four *Spider-Man* films made?

a) Universal Studios Hollywood

b) Paramount Pictures Studio

c) Warner Bros Studios Burbank

d) Sony Pictures Studios

13. What is the Riddler's name in *Batman Returns*?

a) Oswald Cobblepot

b) Edward Nigma

c) Max Shrek

d) Alfred Pennyworth

14. Who portrayed the feline villain in *Catwoman* (2004)?

a) Carmen Electra

b) Michelle Pfeiffer

c) Jessica Biel

d) Halle Berry

15. Name the actor that has starred in both *Star Trek* and *X-Men* films.

a) Bruce Willis

b) Ian McKellan

c) Hugh Jackman

d) Patrick Stewart

16. Which character did Vin Diesel voice in *Guardians of the Galaxy*?

a) Groot

b) Rocky

c) Drax

d) Corpsman Dey

17. Who was the first well-known super soldier?

a) The Hulk

b) Captain America

c) Iron Man

d) Thor

18. What is Hawkeye's preferred weapon of choice?

a) Sword

b) Vision Heat

c) Lightning Bolt

d) Bow and Arrow

19. True or False: Fantastic Four actually has five members.

20. What is the name of Tony Stark's assistant who eventually becomes the CEO of Stark Enterprises?

* * *

QUIZ #1 ANSWERS

1. Catwoman

2. True

3. "This isn't freedom. This is fear."

4. c) 10

5. "And you'll never have to."

6. a) 1989

7. True

8. True

9. The Book of Erebus

10. "We'll see about that."

11. False

12. a) Universal Studios Hollywood

13. b) Edward Nigma

14. d) Halle Berry

15. d) Patrick Stewart

16. a) Groot

17. b) Captain America

18. d) Bow and Arrow

19. False

20. Pepper Potts

* * *

QUIZ #2 QUESTIONS

1. True or False. Wolverine was born as James Howlett Hudson.

2. Who is in a relationship with her team member, Colossus?

a) Rogue

b) Storm

c) Jean Grey

d) Kitty Pryde

3. One of the founding X-Men, Dr. Hank McCoy, is a mutant possessing animal-like strength and agility. Despite being covered in _____ fur and resembling, a ferocious, beast, he possesses an astounding, intellect and superb wit.

4. What is Captain America's real name?

a) Max Eisenhardt

b) Steve Rogers

c) Scott Summers

d) Charles Francis

5. 5.Who has ability to charge inanimate objects with kinetic energy, causing them to explode?

a) Apocalypse

b) Doctor Strange

c) Gambit

d) Deadpool

6. Complete this line from *Superman* (1978). Superman: "Easy, miss. I've got you." Lois:"You've got me? Who's got_____!?"

7. What is the name of the duck who makes a cameo in *Guardians of the Galaxy*?

8. True or False. In Superman (1978). Clark Kent and Superman's hair part on opposite sides.

9. What popular actor portrays The Riddler in *Batman Returns*?

10. Which actor portrays Jor-El in the *Superman* film?

a) Marlon Brando

b) Gene Hackman

c) Christopher Reeve

d) Ned Beatty

11. True or False. *Superman II* is a British-American superhero film directed by Richard Lester and based on the DC Comics character Superman.

12. August "Gus" Gorman is a bumbling computer genius who works for _____?

a) Ross Webster

b) Clark Kent

c) Lana Lang

d) Perry White

13. Which fictional super villain appears in the *Batman* film?

a) Poison Ivy

b) Riddler

c) Scarecrow

d) The Joker

14. Who directed and produced *Batman Returns*?

a) Tim Burton

b) Jim Wynorski

c) Danny Cannon

d) Tim Pope

15. True or False. Alex Hyde-White in the *Fantastic Four* (unreleased film199appears as Victor Von Doom /Dr. Doom.

16. Who portrayed Bruce Wayne /Batman in the movie *Batman Forever*?

a) Val Kilmer

b) Christian Bale

c) George Clooney

d) Michael Keaton

17. In the movie *Batman & Robin*, Chris O'Donnell is Robin aka _____?

a) Dick Grayson

b) James Gordon

c) Alfred Pennyworth

d) James Gordon

18. True or False. Blade is a 19American superhero film based on the Marvel Comics character of the same name.

19. Who is a Canadian mutant who makes a living in cage fights and has lived for fifteen years without memory of who he really is?

a) Wolverine

b) Magneto

c) Professor X

d) Cyclops

20. Who is a Blade's human mentor in the movie *Blade II*?

a) Abraham Whistler

b) Reinhardt

c) Eli Damaskinos

d) Snowman

* * *

QUIZ #2 ANSWERS

1. True

2. d) Kitty Pryde

3. blue

4. b) Steve Rogers

5. c) Gambit

6. "you"

7. Howard

8. True

9. Jim Carrey

10. a) Marlon Brando

11. True

12. a) Ron Webster

13. d) The Joker

14. a) Tim Burton

15. False

16. a) Val Kilmer

17. a) Dick Grayson

18. True

19. a) Wolverine

20. a) Abraham Whistler

* * *

QUIZ #3 QUESTIONS

1. What year was *X2: X-Men United* released to major movie theatres?

a) 2003

b) 1997

c) 1991

d) 1985

2. Who was exposed to a large amount of gamma radiations in an accident in his lab?

a) Matt Murdock /Daredevil

b) Peter Parker /Spider-Man

c) Dr. Reed Richards/ Mister Fantastic

d) Dr. Bruce Banner/ Hulk

3. Who is hired by Kingpin to kill Nikolas and Elektra Natchios in the movie *Daredevil*?

a) Bullseye

b) Ani-Man

c) Cobra

d) Doctor Doom

4. Name team members of the *Guardians of the Galaxy* (2014).

5. True or False. *Batman v Superman: Dawn of Justice* (2016) is the direct sequel to *Man of Steel* 2013.

6. True or False. Dr. Otto Octavius / Doctor Octopus / Doc Ock became insane after his failure to create a self-sustaining fusion reactor in the move *Spider-Man 2*.

7. Who is a mysterious man who trains Bruce in the martial arts by initially posing as a subservient member of the League of Shadows?

a) Henri Ducard /Ra's al Ghul

b) Dr. Jonathan Crane

c) Carmine Falcone

d) William Earle

8. In the movie *X-Men: The Last Stand*, Professor Charles Xavier and Erik Lehnsherr meet young _____ at her parents' house where they invite her to join their school.

a) Jean Grey

b) Rogue

c) Dr. Hank McCoy/Beast

d) Kitty Pryde/Shadowcat

9. Which actor is a psychotic criminal mastermind who portrays himself as an "agent of chaos" in the movie *The Dark Knight*?

a) Heath Ledger

b) Aaron Eckhart

c) Ron Dean

d) Gary Oldman

10. True or False. Lt. Colonel James "Rhodey" Rhodes is an industrialist, genius inventor, a consummate playboy and the CEO of Stark Industries.

11. Who directed the 2006 movie *Superman Returns*?

a) Michael Bay

b) Harry Styles

c) Tim Burton

d) Bryan Singer

12. True or False

    In *Spider-Man 3* (2007) all of the screams made by Kirsten Dunst were recycled from *Spider- Man 2* (2004).

13. In *The Avengers (2012)*, which superhero uttered the phrase "Let's just not come in tomorrow"?

a) Captain America

b) Thor

c) Iron Man

d) Black Widow

14. Who was the female lead in the 2011 film, *Green Lantern*?

a) Scarlett Johansson

b) Megan Fox

c) Blake Lively

d) Michelle Pfeiffer

15. Fill in the blank. The Penguin from *Batman Returns* says:

    "Why is there always someone who brings _____ to a speech?"

16. In *Captain America: The Winter Soldier*, what is the full name of Steve Rogers (Chris Evans) childhood friend, now known as "The Winter Soldier"?

a) James Buchanan Barnes

b) Bucky James Barnes

c) James Barnham Buchanan

d) James Barnham Bucky

17. *Catwoman* was released in what year by Warner Bros.?

a) 2004

b) 1999

c) 1994

d) 1989

18. What actor portrays Hannibal King in the movie *Blade: Trinity*?

a) Ryan Reynolds

b) Dominic Purcell

c) Kris Kristofferson

d) Wesley Snipes

19. Fill in the blank from 2011's *Thor*. "You're big, but I've fought_____."

20. True or False. Original Hulk TV actor Lou Ferrigno had a cameo in the 2008 *Incredible Hulk* film.

* * *

QUIZ # 3 ANSWERS

1. a) 2003

2. d) Dr. Bruce Banner/Hulk

3. a) Bullseye

4. Star Lord, Gamora, Drax, Groot, Rocket Raccoon

5. True

6. True

7. a) Henri Ducard /Ra's al Ghul

8. a) Jean Grey

9. a) Heath Ledger

10. False

11. d) Bryan Singer

12. True

13. c) Iron Man

14. c) Blake Lively

15. "eggs and tomatoes"

16. a) James Buchanan Barnes

17. a) Catwoman

18. a) Ryan Reynolds

19. "bigger"

20. True

* * *

QUIZ #4 QUESTIONS

1. True or False. Loki and Thor are cousins.

2. Stan Lee made a cameo appearance as Hugh Hefner in what *Avengers'* film?

3. Who is Thor's adoptive brother and archenemy?

a) Ares

b) Destroyer

c) Galactus

d) Loki

4. Who is Hitler's head of advanced weaponry and commander of the terrorist organization Hydra in *Captain America: The First Avenger*?

a) Red skull

b) King Cobra

c) The Grand Director

d) Winter Soldier

5. Who is a former Los Angeles gang member who can summon flames in the movie *Suicide Squad*?

a) El Diablo

b) Killer Croc

c) Rick Flag

d) Deadshot

6. Which of these actors didn't play more than one movie superhero?

a) Chris Pratt

b) Chris Evans

c) Ryan Reynolds

d) Brandon Routh

7. Which of these *Spider-Man* villains never appeared in a movie?

a) Rhino

b) Lizard

c) Kraven

d) Hobgoblin

8. In how many movies does Hugh Jackman appear as Wolverine?

9. True or False. In the 2009 *The Watchmen* film, all of the U.S flags have 51 stars because of the film's alternate history. The 51st state is South Korea.

10. In the 1998 film *Blade*, what actor portrays the half-vampire, half-mortal man who becomes the protector of the mortal race?

a) Eddie Murphy

b) Will Smith

c) Wesley Snipes

d) Chris Tucker

11. In the 2008 *Iron Man* film, what actor played the role of Jim Rhodes (Rhodey)?

a) Terrence Howard

b) Don Cheadle

c) Martin Freeman

d) Will Smith

12. Who directed the 2002 *Spider-Man* film?

13. Which of these isn't Professor X's ability?

a) Mind control

b) Telepathy

c) Telekinesis

d) Astral projection

e) Memory manipulation

14. Which movie didn't have a reference in 2016's *Deadpool*?

a) *X-Men Origins: Wolverine*

b) *Green Lantern*

c) *Thor*

d) *Spider-Man*

15. What is the name of Tony Stark's company?

16. Blackheart is the name of the villain in which of the following movies?

a) *Blade: Trinity*

b) *Ghost Rider*

c) *Thor: The Dark World*

d) *Electra*

17. What is the name of Iron Man's personal A.I. assistant?

a) Alfred

b) Yinsen

c) J.A.R.V.I.S.

d) Obadiah

18. Which metal is Captain America's shield made of?

a) Adamantium

b) Titanium

c) Vibranium

d) Kryptonite

19. What is the name of the alien species which invaded Earth in the 2012 *Avengers* film?

a) Skrulls

b) The Kree

c) Parallax

d) Chitauri

20. Who is the main villain in the *Guardians of the Galaxy* 2014?

a) Nebula

b) Ronan

c) Tanos

d) Dr. Doom

* * *

QUIZ # 4 ANSWERS

1. False

2. Iron Man

3. d) Loki

4. a) Red Skull

5. a) El Diablo

6. d) Brandon Routh

7. c) Kraven and d) Hobgoblin

8. Eight

9. False

10. c) Wesley Snipes

11. a) Terrence Howard

12. Sam Rami

13. c) Telekinesis

14. c) Thor

15. Stark Industries

16. b) Ghost Rider

17. c) J.A.R.V.I.S.

18. c) Vibranium

19. d) Chitauri

20. d) Dr. Doom

* * *

QUIZ #5 QUESTIONS

1. How many movies has the character Nick Fury appeared?

2. How many films has Iron Man/Tony Stark appeared?

3. Name the team members of the *Avengers* film.

4. True or False: Eric Bana Portrayed the title character in the *The Incredible Hulk*.

5. What is the name of Magneto's organization in first *X-Men* trilogy?

6. Which of the following heroes was not a member of the *X-Men: First Class* team?

a) Mystique
b) Havok
c) Banshee
d) Emma Frost

7. Where was most of the footage filmed for *Spider-Man* (2002)?

8. What young female villain from Batman's world makes her debut in the *Suicide Squad*?

9. Which of these superheroes was blinded as a child?

a) Falcon

b) Night Owl

c) Daredevil

d) Hawkeye

10. Which of these characters were portrayed by more than one actor on film?

a) Quicksilver

b) Magneto

c) Electra

d) Black Widow

11. Which of these characters never appeared in *Batman* movies?

a) Batgirl

b) Nightwing

c) Victor Zsasz

d) Batwoman

12. Which member of *The Avengers* team appears in *Iron Man 2*?

13. Who did Mystique try to assassinate in *X-Men: Days of Future Past*?

a) Magneto

b) Professor X

c) Bolivar Trask

d) President Nixon

14. Betty Ross is the love interest of the main hero in which movie?

a) *The Incredible Hulk* (2008)

b) *Ghost Rider* (2007)

c) *Man of Steel* (2013)

d) *Thor* (2011)

15. Who directed the film, *The Fantastic Four*?

a) Kenneth Branagh

    b) Oley Sassone

    c) *Tim Story*

    d) *Josh Trank*

16. How much weight did Seth Rogen lose for his role in *The Green Hornet* (2011)?

    a) 20 pounds

    b) 25 pounds

    c) *30 pounds*

    d) *35 pounds*

17. True or False. *Guardians of the Galaxy* was based on a DC comic book series.

18. Fill in the blank from the Joker in *The Dark Knight*.

    The Joker: "If you're good at something, Never _____."

19. In the film *The Wolverine* (Yashida gives Wolverine a sword with six letters engraved on it. What does it say?

    a) "Never Trust, Never Lie, Never Betray"

    b) "Never Died, Never Aged, Never Destroyed"

c) "Never Wound, Never Harm, Never Kill"

d) "Never Found, Never Lost, Never Lived"

20. What is the name Wonder Woman uses in Superman v Batman: Dawn of Justice?

* * *

QUIZ #5 ANSWERS

1. 8

2. 7

3. Iron Man, Captain America, The Hulk, Thor, Black Widow and Hawkeye.

4. False

5. Brotherhood of Mutants

6. d) Emma Frost

7. Los Angeles and New York City

8. Harley Quinn

9. c) Daredevil

10. a) and b)

11. b) Nightwing c) Victor Zsasz d) Batwoman

12. Black Widow

13. c) Bolivar Trask

14. a) The Incredible Hulk

15. b) Oley Sassone

16. c) pounds

17. False

18. "Do it for free."

19. b) "Never Died, Never Aged, Never Destroyed"

20. Diana Prince

* * *

QUIZ #6 QUESTIONS

1. Which newspaper does the *Spider-Man* Peter Parker work for?

a) The Daily Planet
b) The Daily Bugle
c) The Daily Telegraph
d) The Daily Journal

2. In *Spider-Man* (2002), what character says, "Remember, with great power, come great responsibility."

3. Name the actor who portrays Loki in the two *Thor* and *Avengers* films?

4. True or False. Actor Jeremy Renner (Hawkeye) trained for the role with Olympic archers.

5. Name the famed Batman villain who was the judge in *The Dark Knight Rises*.

6. Fill in the blank from Thor (2011).
   Loki: "You know, it all makes sense now, why you favored Thor all these years, because no

matter how much you claim to love me, you could never have a Frost Giant sitting on the throne of _____."

7. Halle Berry won a 'Razzle' for her performance in *Catwoman* (2004). She then became one of how many to have won both an Oscar and a Razzle?

a) 3

b) 4

c) 5

d) 6

8. True or False. *Watchmen* (features a classic villain.

9. There is a difference between the two popular *Spider-Man* actors Toby Maguire and Andrew Garfield costumes. What is it?

10. What color is the Black Widow's hair in The Avengers (and Age of Ultron (2015)?

11. Fill in the blank from 1997's *Batman & Robin*. Robin: "I want a car. Chicks dig a car."

Batman: "That's why _____ works alone."

12. True or False: While filming *Daredevil* (2003), during a fight scene, Ben Affleck accidently kicked Jennifer Garner in the head and she actually passed out.

13. What is the name of the stone creature Thor fights in *Thor: The Dark World*?

14. What is the title of the fourth *Avengers* film?

a) *Avengers Infinity*

b) *Avengers: Infinity War*

c) *Avengers Infinity War Part 2*

d) *Avengers Infinity and Beyond*

15. Fill in the blank. In *Captain America: Civil War*, Iron Man tells Captain to "stay down" and the Captain replies, "_____"

16. True or False. *Captain America: The Civil War* is the longest Marvel film made to date.

17. Where was *Thor: The Dark World* filmed?

a) New Zealand

b) Australia

c) Iceland

d) Norway

18. True or False. In *Batman Returns*, Annette Bening was the director's first choice to portray Catwoman.

19. What is the title of the movie released on the 75th Anniversary of Superman?

20. What was the *X-Men: Apocalypse* original movie title?

* * *

QUIZ #6 ANSWERS

1. The Daily Bugle

2. Uncle Ben

3. Tom Hiddleston

4. True

5. Scarecrow

6. Asgard

7. d) 6

8. True

9. Their webbing. (Maguire's Spider-Man has organic webbing while Garfield's updated Spider-Man uses web shooters to fit how it worked in the comics).

10. red

11. Superman

12. False (Jennifer Garner accidentally kicked Ben Affleck so hard in the head that he briefly blacked out)

13. Kronan

14. b)

15. "I can do this all day."

16. True

17. c) Iceland

18. True

19. Man of Steel

20. Age of Apocalypse

* * *

QUIZ #7 QUESTIONS

1. What renders Superman helpless?

2. In the movie versions of *The Hulk* and *The Avengers*, what is the real name of the big green superhero?

a) Benjamin Grimm
b) Bruce Banner
c) T'Challa
d) Reed Richards

3. What is the name of the actress that portrays Jean Grey in *X-Men: Apocalypse*?

a) Jennifer Lawrence
b) Sophie Turner
c) Kristen Stewart
d) Dakota Fanning

4. Peter Parker's love interest in Spider-Man was this character.

a) Betty Ross
b) Pepper Potts

c) Mary Jane Watson

d) Jane Foster

5. True or False: *X-Men*'s Mystique has also appeared in the *Fantastic Four* movie.

6. Which superhero film does villain Poison Ivy appear in?

a) *Spider-Man II*

b) Superman II

c) Batman Returns

d) Batman and R*obin*

7. Villain Dr. Otto Octavius appears in what superhero movie?

8. True or False. On the set of *The Avengers* (2012), unknown to his co-stars, Robert Downey Jr. kept food hidden everywhere. When Tony Stark offers Bruce Banner (Mark Ruffalo) blueberries, that was actually an unscripted moment.

9. Which actor portrayed The Joker in *The Dark Knight* (2008)?

a) Robert Downey Jr.

b) Christian Bale

c) Heath Ledger

d) Hugh Jackman

10. Which young actor played this *Spider-Man* in 2002?

a) Freddie Prince Jr.

b) Toby Maguire

c) Logan Lerman

d) Orlando Bloom

11. What movie superhero said "It's not who I am underneath, but what I do that defines me."

a) Superman

b) Batman

c) Spider-Man

d) Captain America

12. What is the name of the actor that portrayed Hal Jordan in *Green Lantern* (2011)

a) Ryan Reynolds

b) Nicolas Cage

c) Joel Edgerton

d) Shia LaBeouf

13. Who directed the *Superman* which starred Christopher Reeve?

a) Sam Rami

b) Richard Lester

c) Richard Donner

d) Gene Hackman

14. What actor portrayed *Deadpool* (2016)?

a) Ben Affleck

b) Ryan Reynolds

c) Henry Cavill

d) Mark Ruffalo

15. What movie superhero or villain said "Mankind is not evil, just... uninformed."

a) Thor

b) Iron Man

c) Loki

d) Professor X

16. In *The Fantastic Four* (2004), what are Johnny Storm's and Ben Grimm's professions?

a) Teachers

b) Astronauts

c) Doctors

d) Construction Workers

17. In *Superman Returns* (what is the name of Clark Kent's adopted mother?

a) Marie Kent

b) Mara Kent

c) Martha Kent

d) Mary Kent

18. Name the actor that portrays Johnny Blaze *in Ghost Rider* (2007)?

19. So far, how many actors have played the Hulk in movies since 2003?

a) 4

b) 2

c) 3

d) 1

20. What is the name of the Green Hornet's (side-kick?

* * *

QUIZ #7 ANSWERS

1. Kyptonite

2. b) Bruce Banner

3. b) Sophie Turner

4. c) Mary Jane Watson

5. False

6. d) Batman and Robin

7. Spider-Man 2

8. True

9. c) Heath Ledger

10. b) Toby Maguire

11. b) Batman

12. a) Ryan Reynolds

13. c) Richard Donner

14. b) Ryan Reynolds

15. d) Professor X

16. b) Astronauts

17. c) Martha Kent

18. Nicolas Cage

19. c) Eric Bana, Edward Norton and Mark Ruffalo

20. Kato

* * *

QUIZ #8 QUESTIONS

1. At the beginning of *Captain America: Civil War*, what year is depicted?

a) 1992

b) 1991

c) 1989

d) 1990

2. In *Spider-Man* the character Eddie Brock Jr.. turns into what evil villain?

3. In the film, Hulk, scientist Bruce Banner was exposed to what kind of rays?

4. Jessica Alba plays what character in the *Fantastic Four*?

5. In the *X-Men The Last Stand*, who is Jean Grey's fierce alter-ego?

a) The Raven

b) The Canary

c) The Phoenix

    d) The Hawk

6. Wolverine's claws are made from this super strong metal.

    a) Vibranium
    b) Adamantium
    c) Zinc
    d) Titanium

7. What is Deadpool's real name?

8. In *Fantastic Four: Rise of The Silver Surfer* (, what is the name of the actor that plays the Silver Surfer?

9. In the movie *Daredevil*, what was the hero blinded by?

10. True or false. Ed Norton played the character Hulk in the *The Incredible Hulk*

11. Who does Wolverine stab by accident in the *X-Men* film?

a)   Professor X

b)   Cyclops

c)   Jean Grey

d)   Rogue

12. What is the name of the character in the very first *Iron Man film* who was a fellow captive in Afghanistan with Tony Stark?

a)   Iron Monger

b)   War Machine

c)   Razza

d)   Ho Yinsen

13. In *Thor,* what was Doctor Jane Foster and her team studying in New Mexico?

14. In the *Watchmen* movie who does the character Nite Owl Fall in love with?

a)   Wonder Woman

b)   Silk Spectre II

c)   Sally Jupiter

d)   Janey Slater

15. Who is the *Thor* support actress who later became a "Broke Girl" ?

a) Natalie Portman

b) Jamie Alexander

c) Kat Dennings

d) Rene Russo

16. In *Watchmen* what year (in alternative history) is set at the height of the Cold War between the US and Soviet Union?

a) 1987

b) 1986

c) 1985

d) 1984

17. What superhero movie does the villain Blackheart appear in?

a) *Ghost Rider*

b) *The Dark Night*

c) *Spider-Man*

d) *Batman & Robin*

18. Sexy villain Poison Ivy appears in what Batman-themed movie?

a) *The Dark Knight*

b) *Batman & Robin*

c) *Batman Returns*

d) *Batman Forever*

19. In *Batman Forever,* what actor portrays the Bruce Wayne/Batman

a) George Clooney

b) Michael Keaton

c) Val Kilmer

d) Christian Bale

20. True or False. Gene Hackman played Lex Luther in *Superman III*?

* * *

QUIZ #8 ANSWERS

1. b) 1991

2. Venom

3. Gamma Rays

4. Sue Storm

5. c) The Phoenix

6. b) Adamantium

7. Wade Wilson

8. Doug Jones

9. Toxic Waste

10. True

11. Rogue

12. c) Razza

13. Astronomical Anomalies

14. b) Silk Spectre II

15. c) Kat Dennings

16. c) 1985

17. a) Ghost Rider

18. b) Batman & Robin

19. c) Val Kilmer

20. False. Just Superman &

* * *

Thank you for talking the time to read *The Superheroes Movies Trivia Quiz Book*. If you enjoyed it, please tell your superhero liked-minded friends or post a positive review online. Positive word of mouth is an author's best friend.

Follow me on <u>Twitter.com/themacwire</u> and join me on <u>Facebook.com/macassata.</u> See ya online!

* * *

ABOUT THE AUTHOR

Always fascinated by pop culture, M.A. Cassata's diverse writing career has included such national print publications as *Variety*, *Hollywood Reporter*, *Rolling Stone*, *USA Today*, *The New York Daily News*, *People Weekly*, and more.

Cassata has penned 20 plusbooks on celebrities including One Direction, Big Time Rush, Cher, Elton John, and Jim Carrey. She is the former Editorial Director at *Popstar! Publications* and continues to contribute to various entertainment-oriented print and online publications. She lives in northern New Jersey and owns the entertainment-based website themacwire.com. For more information on the author's complete works visit Macassata.com.

* * *